sOUND

Hebrews 12:1

For Ella Grace

The music to my ears.

A life that makes a sound

There once was a girl so profound. Her life is one that makes a sound.

You see sometimes sound

isn't something to hear. A stir in the heart not in the ear.

It's not just about noise it's also effect. Causing

those who experience it to remember what they too often neglect.

From the day she was born
it was clear she was unique.
Just as every new parent
should think.

Every milestone of life met without delay.

All nearly changed one fateful winter day.

The world went dark,
the lowest of low.
The Earth stood still as she
was rushed through the snow.

Her life within minutes of drifting away

with the help of great heroes she decided to stay.

Given a
one percent chance
she used as a prod.
Her first lesson to share
don't live life by the odds.

From there it became apparent another thing she had to share.

She is one of
those rare souls
that makes
things better
just by
being there.

Even with one side of her body weakened
to pity herself she did not waste the time.
Instead she seemed to say I can do anything
you can do because my other side works just fine.

The hope that lives within her heart
there's no way she'll submit.
Once she sets her mind to task
there's no such thing as quit.

Dance Trophies

Art Project

Scholastic Awards

When the dark times come
she looks for the light.
You see the stars shine the brightest
in the darkest of night.

She taught her dad
to believe in miracles
and her sister
to sing and dance.
She even gets her mom
to cut a rug
when she gets
the chance.

Her story inspired so many
who held her in thoughts and prayers.
It's a powerful thing in times like these
to see people truly care.

You see her sound is her example that echoes to this day.
If only we'd all grab hold of life and live it in such a way.

So open your eyes to your surroundings.

Become aware of the little things.

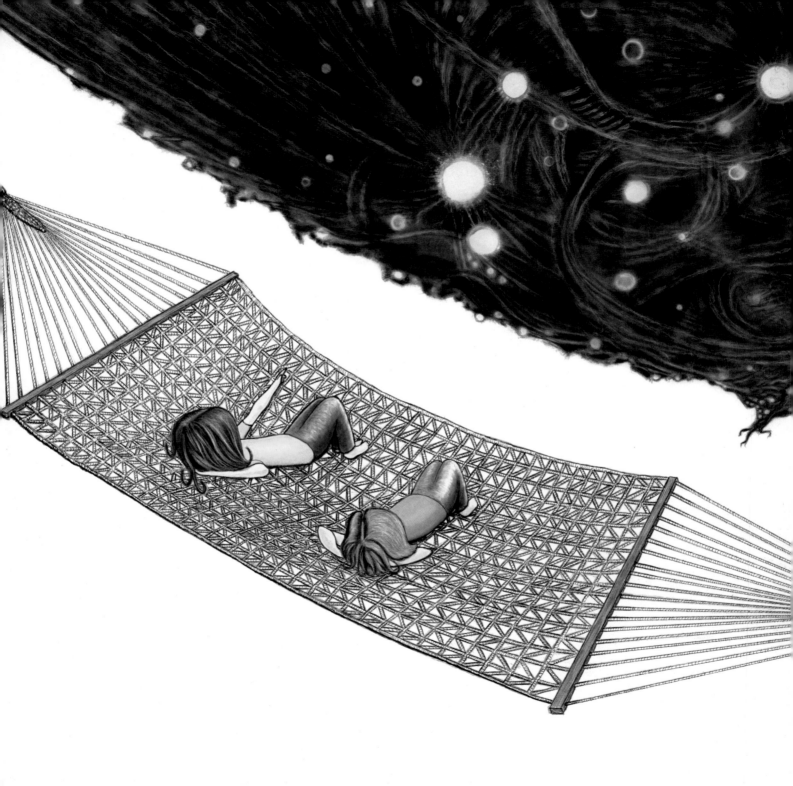

Allow yourself to be inspired.

Then be inspiring.

All of the
wonderful
sounds such
as this.

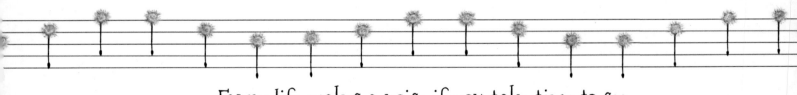

Every life makes a noise if you take time to see.

What has yours been, and now what will it be?

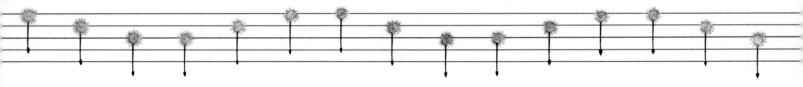

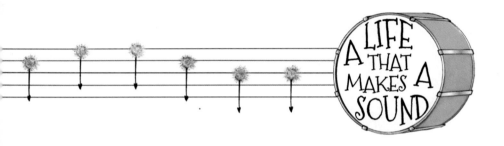

SOUND

Made in the USA
Columbia, SC
06 July 2022